Active
EARTH

First published in 2012 by Miles Kelly
Publishing Ltd, Harding's Barn, Bardfield End
Green, Thaxted, Essex, CM6 3PX, UK

Copyright © Miles Kelly Publishing Ltd 2011

© 2014 Discovery Communications, LLC.
Discovery Explore Your World™ and the
Discovery Explore Your World™ logo are
trademarks of Discovery Communications, LLC,
used under license. All rights reserved.
discoveryuk.com

This edition published in 2014

10 9 8 7 6 5 4 3 2 1

Publishing Director Belinda Gallagher
Creative Director Jo Cowan
Managing Editors Amanda Askew,
  Rosie Neave
Managing Designer Simon Lee
Proofreaders Carly Blake, Claire Philip
Production Manager Elizabeth Collins
Image Manager Liberty Newton
Reprographics Stephan Davis, Thom Allaway

ISBN 978-1-78209-525-5

Printed in China

British Library Cataloguing-in-Publication Data
A catalogue record for this book is available
from the British Library

Made with paper from a sustainable forest

www.mileskelly.net
info@mileskelly.net

ACKNOWLEDGMENTS

The publishers would like to thank the following sources for the use
of their photographs:

KEY Fotolia=F, Frank Lane Picture Agency=FLPA, Getty Images=GI,
istockphoto.com=iS, Minden Pictures=MP, naturepl.com/Nature Picture
Library=NPL, Photolibrary=P, Rex Features=RF, Robert Harding World
Imagery=RHWI, Science Photo Library=SPL, Shutterstock=S
t=top, a=above, b=bottom/below, c=center, l=left, r=right, f=far, m=main,
bg=background

COVER Zastol`skiy Victor Leonidovich/S **1** Albo /F **2** Pedro Nogueira/S
3(bg) Jose AS Reyes/S (strip, left to right) Vulkanette/S, Ulrich Mueller/S,
Scott Prokop/S, Pichugin Dmitry/S, ABC.pics/S **4–5** Adam Jones/SPL
6–7(m) NASA Earth Observatory/SPL, (l) Tony Craddock/SPL, (tr) NASA-JSC-
ES&IA, (frame) Shawn Hine/S, (br) Gordon Garradd/SPL **8–9**(bg) Jose AS
Reyes/S, (m) mangiurea **8**(l) Andrea Danti, (br) George Steinmetz/SPL
9(tl) Vitaly Korovin, (tr) Michael Peuckert/P, (br) Arctic-Images/Corbis
10–11(m) Grant Dixon/MP/FLPA **10**(c) Doug Allan/NPL, (frame)
imagestock/iS, **11**(cr) Galen Rowell/Corbis, (br) Valentyn Volkov/S
12–13(c) Vulkanette/S, (cb) Doug Perrine **12**(bl) Peter Oxford/NPL/RF
13(tr) Alexander Gatsenko/S **14** Carlyn Iverson/SPL **15**(t) Michael
Krabs/Imagebroker/FLPA, (cr) Nadezda/S, (b) Dr. Richard Roscoe, Visuals
Unlimited/SPL **16–17**(bg) KPA/Zuma/RF **16**(cl) Gary Hinks/SPL, (br) Sipa
Press/RF **17**(tr) UC Regents, Natl. Information Service For Earthquake
Engineering/SPL, (cl) Corbis, (br) dpa/Corbis **18–19**(water bg) Dudarev
Mikhail/S, (bl) Aaron Amat/S, (tl) Frank Siteman/Science Faction,
(cl) Jacques Jangoux/Peter Arnold Images/P, (cr) Kevin Schafer/MP/FLPA,
(tr) Kevin Schafer/MP/FLPA, (br) Planetobserver/SPL **20**(bg) Jack
Dykinga/NPL, (c) Scott Prokop/S, (b) Konstantin Sutyagin/GI
21(bg) ImageState, (sign tr) Steve Collender/S and dusan964/S,
(m) Albo/F, (sign b) Lou Oates/S, (b) Grant Dixon/MP/FLPA
22–3(m) Bernhard Edmaier/SPL, (bl) Marcos Brindicci/Reuters/Corbis,
(paper tr) pdtnc/F, (br) Colin Monteath/P **24–5**(m) Steven
Kazlowski/Science Faction/Corbis **24**(c) KeystoneUSA-ZUMA/RF,
(paper cl) Alexey Khromushin/F, (sign br) marekuliasz/S

25(sign tl) Steve Collender/S, (sign tr) maxkovalev/S, (cl) Ashley
Cooper/Corbis, (cr) Carsten Peter/Speleoresearch & Films/GI, (sign bl) Lou
Oates/S, (br) Tony Waltham/RHWI/Corbis **26–7**(bg) Mirek Hejnicki/S,
sspopov/S, SeDmi/S, kilukilu/S and leolintang/S; (objects on conveyor belt,
l–r, t–b) Serhiy Shullye/S, Outsider/S, E.R.Degginger/SPL, Picsfive/S, Denis
Selivanov/S, Keith Wilson/S, Konovalikov Andrey/S, Alexander Kalina/S,
Bragin Alexey/S, Jean-Claude Revy, ISM/SPL, Kamil Krzaczynski/epa/Corbis,
Juri/S, dslaven/S, Krasowit/S, Jens Mayer/S, stocksnapp/S, Maria
Brzostowska/F, Steve Vidler/P, Jason Reed/Reuters/Corbis; (tr) Jon T.
Fritz/MCT **28**(tr frame) diak/S, (tl) NPL, (gold plate) Alaettin YildIrim/S,
(cr) Argus/S, (bl) Jeffrey L. Rotman **29**(tr) Victor Habbick Visions/SPL,
(cl) NPL/RF, (laptop bl) Edhar/S, (bl) Dr Ken Macdonald/SPL, (br) Jamie
Cross/S **30–1**(bg) Planetobserver/SPL **30**(t–b, l–r) John Wollwerth/S, Mike
Hollingshead/Science Faction/Corbis, Jim Reed/Jim Reed Photography –
Severe &/Corbis, dswebb/iS **31**(t–b, l–r) Caitlin Mirra/S, jam4travel/S,
Carsten Peter/GI, Irwin Thompson/Dallas Morning News/Corbis **32**(m) Gene
Rhoden/P, (c) 2010 Gallo Images/GI, (bl) AFP/GI, (br) Jim Reed/FLPA
33(tl) Olivier Vandeginste/SPL, (tr) mtkang/S, (c) Ivan Cholakov Gostock-
dot-net/S, (b) AFP/GI **34–5**(m) Scott Warren/P **34**(bl) Joel Blit/S,
(br) Steve Collender/S **35**(bl) Picimpact/Corbis, (c) Brandelet/S
36–7(tm) Ward Kennan/P, (t, l–r) Dan Burton/NPL, AlaskaStock/P,
Planetary Visions Ltd/SPL, (bm) Juniors Bildarchiv/P, (b, l–r) George
Steinmetz/Corbis, Frans Lanting/Corbis, Planetary Visions Ltd/SPL
38(bg) Sasha Buzko, (tl) Tischenko Irina/S, (cl) Anan Kaewkhammul/S,
(cr) Mikhail/S, (frame, bl) imagestock, (bl) Kordcom Kordcom/P
39(tl) Michael Freeman/Corbis, (frame c) Cre8tive Images/S,
(c) T Carrafa/Newspix/RF, (r) Anan Kaewkhammul/S

All other photographs are from: Corel, digitalSTOCK, digitalvision,
Dreamstime.com, Fotolia.com, iStockphoto.com, John Foxx, PhotoAlto,
PhotoDisc, PhotoEssentials, PhotoPro, Stockbyte

Every effort has been made to acknowledge the source and copyright
holder of each picture. The publishers apologise for any unintentional
errors or omissions.

Active EARTH

Camilla de la Bedoyere
Consultant: Steve Parker

Miles Kelly

CONTENTS

◀ The pattern of lines in this rock face in the Paria Canyon-Vermilion Cliffs Wilderness, on the border of Utah and Arizona, U.S., is caused by layers of compressed sandstone worn smooth by glacier erosion.

Visitors from SPACE

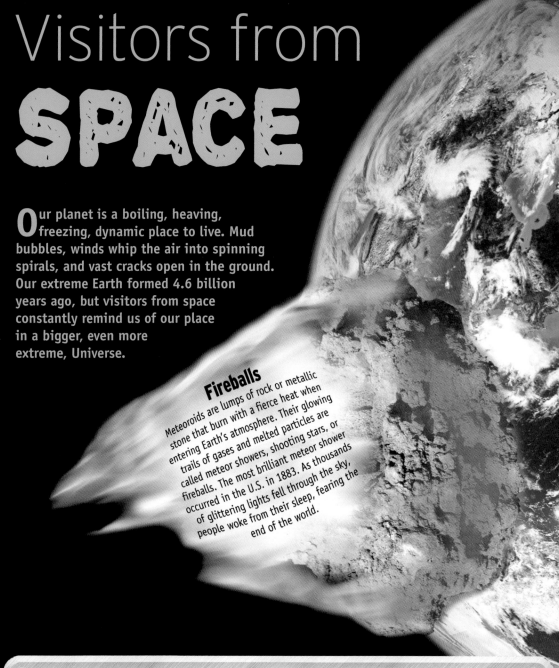

Our planet is a boiling, heaving, freezing, dynamic place to live. Mud bubbles, winds whip the air into spinning spirals, and vast cracks open in the ground. Our extreme Earth formed 4.6 billion years ago, but visitors from space constantly remind us of our place in a bigger, even more extreme, Universe.

Fireballs

Meteoroids are lumps of rock or metallic stone that burn with a fierce heat when entering Earth's atmosphere. Their glowing trails of gases and melted particles are called meteor showers, shooting stars, or fireballs. The most brilliant meteor shower occurred in the U.S. in 1883. As thousands of glittering lights fell through the sky, people woke from their sleep, fearing the end of the world.

Total wipeout!

The cataclysmic K-P Event occurred 65.5 million years ago. The impact of a meteorite crash near Chicxulub, Mexico, threw dust and rock into the air, blocking sunlight and affecting the climate for 10,000 years. Scientists believe this caused the extinction of about 80 percent of animal species, including dinosaurs.

If another giant meteorite heads toward Earth, it could raise the temperature of the air beneath it to 100,000°F (about 60,000°C)—ten times hotter than the Sun's surface. The impact could blast 250 cu mi (about 1,000 cu km) of rock and gas into the air, and produce shock waves that trigger earthquakes.

Polar light show

Some of Earth's most staggering sights are the aurorae, when night skies around the North and South poles are lit up by ghostly curtains of light that sweep across the darkness. This extreme effect is caused by the action of Earth's magnetic field on streams of particles that have been carried from the Sun on a solar wind.

▲ *Aurora australis* (Southern Lights), seen from the International Space Station (ISS).

THE LARGEST METEORITE CRATER IS AT VREDEFORT IN SOUTH AFRICA. IT HAS A DIAMETER OF 180 MI (ABOUT 300 KM).

▼ Comet Hyakutake, seen on March 21, 1996.

Burning ice

Comets are chunks of ice, rock, and frozen gases that become superheated as they near the Sun, and produce flares of bright light. In 1996 the path of the comet Hyakutake took it close to Earth—a mere 9 million mi (15 million km) away—and it became one of the brightest celestial events for 200 years. The comet is now heading toward the edges of the Solar System and won't be seen again for 72,000 years.

▲ U.S. astronaut James Irwin described Earth from space as "a sparkling blue-and-white jewel."

CRACKING Up

At Earth's center, temperatures reach a staggering 9,800°F (about 5,400°C). Like a mighty engine room, this hot core powers vast movements of rock and causes the planet's outer crust to break into sections and move. The result is an array of awesome seismic events, from the creation of mountains to earthquakes in all their destructive power.

TECTONIC PLATES

North American Plate

Eurasian Plate

Philippine Plate

Australian Plate

Solid inner core made from iron and nickel

Liquid outer core

Heat from the core passes through the almost-solid lower mantle

Material in the upper mantle can flow slightly

Pressure from the mantle can cause the rocky crust to crack

The Pacific Ring of Fire

Thanks to its fearsome history, the world's most violent area of seismic activity is known as the Pacific Ring of Fire. With more than 75 percent of the world's volcanoes and active plate movements, this region is responsible for much of the planet's geology, including the Andes, Mount St. Helens, the islands of Japan, and Krakatau, one of the planet's most explosive volcanoes.

◄ Volcanic steam escapes from a vent in Antarctica.

▲ Inside Earth, there are layers of different material, heated by the core.

A growing ocean

The Atlantic Ocean conceals the world's longest mountain chain—the Mid-Atlantic Ridge. These massive underwater peaks create a ridge 10,000 mi (about 16,000 km) in length, where plates meet over a hot region of mantle. Lava adds to the crust, building up the plates and forcing them further apart.

▶ Cracks and tears appear in Iceland, following the line of the Mid-Atlantic Ridge.

Eurasian Plate

Arabian Plate

African Plate

Indian Plate

South American Plate

Nazca Plate

◀ In 2010, Iceland's Eyjafjallajökull volcano wreaked travel havoc when it spewed plumes of dust across the North Atlantic Ocean and Europe. The highest plume was almost 7 mi (11 km) high and pumped out thousands of tons of ash, grounding planes for a week.

Island of fire and ice

Iceland is an island of extremes. Largely covered in glaciers, it was formed from active volcanoes on the Mid-Atlantic Ridge. About one third of all Earth's lava flows in the last 2,000 years have occurred there.

Mightiest

MOUNTAIN

The Himalayas are not just the biggest mountain range on land, they are also one of the youngest at just 50 million years old. Mount Everest, the highest peak of the Himalayas and in the world, is known as *Chomolungma* in Tibet, and *Sagarmatha* in Nepal.

THE SOUTHEAST RIDGE IS THE MOST CLIMBED ROUTE. IT IS REACHED FROM NEPAL.

MOUNT EVEREST SUMMIT
29,035 ft (8,850 m)

DEATH ZONE
Surviving at altitudes above 26,000 ft is tough, due to low oxygen and freezing temperatures. Climbers who die are often left on the mountain. Eventually, sometimes years later, their frozen bodies are removed for proper burial.

CAMP 4
26,000 ft (8,000 m)

CAMP 1
20,000 ft (6,000 m)

Climbers use a ladder to traverse the crevasse at Khumbu Icefall.

KHUMBU ICEFALL
The Khumbu Icefall must be crossed with the aid of ladders and ropes—it is one of the most dangerous parts of the route.

TIMELINE

1841
The location of peak "b" (as Everest was then known) is recorded by Sir George Everest, Surveyor General of India.

1856
Height of peak "b" is calculated as 29,002 ft (8,840 m).

1865
Peak "b" is renamed Mount Everest.

1924
First attempt at climbing Everest fails, though one climber reaches 28,126 ft (8,570 m).

1953
Edmund Hillary (from New Zealand) and Tenzing Norgay (from Nepal) are the first people to reach Everest's summit on May 29.

2007
Retired Japanese teacher Katsusuke Yanagisawa scales Everest at age 71.

BASE CAMP
On the Khumbu Glacier at 17,700 ft (5,400 m), climbers get used to the altitude before ascending.

TOP 5 PEAKS

EVEREST
29,035 ft
(8,850 m)

K2
28,251 ft
(8,611 m)

KANGCHENJUNGA
28,169 ft
(8,586 m)

LHOTSE
27,940 ft
(8,516 m)

MAKALU
27,838 ft
(8,485 m)

AFTER YEARS OF DISAGREEMENTS ABOUT **EVEREST'S HEIGHT**, CHINA AND NEPAL AGREE IT IS **29,029** FT (8,848 M) HIGH, INCLUDING 13 FT (4 M) OF SNOW, BUT THE NATIONAL GEOGRAPHIC SOCIETY CLAIMS IT IS **29,035** FT (8,850 M) TALL.

NUPTSE (peak)
25,790 ft (7,860 m)

LHOTSE (peak)
27,940 ft (8,516 m)

CAMP 3
24,500 ft
(7,500 m)

GENEVA SPUR
Climbers use ropes to scramble over this raised black rock.

CAMP 2
21,300 ft
(6,500 m)

WHAT RUBBISH!

Everest can now claim fame as the world's highest garbage heap. Tourists and climbers are responsible for leaving plastic bottles, food packaging, tents, and even oxygen tanks on the mountain.

Climbers use iceaxes and crampons—metal spikes attached to boots—to scale vertical sheets of ice.

Ultimate
VOLCANO

Earth's crust breaks open and molten rock, ash, and toxic gases spew out of the vent. The awesome force of a volcanic eruption like this hints at the incredible temperatures and pressures that exist far beneath the surface. But what exactly happens to create the ultimate volcano?

▶ In 1980, Mount St. Helens erupted. The top 4,600 ft (1,400 m) of the volcano was destroyed.

VOLCANIC ERUPTIONS ARE MEASURED ON THE VOLCANIC EXPLOSIVITY INDEX (VEI), WHICH RANGES FROM "GENTLE" TO "MEGA-COLOSSAL."

Lava

Rock that has literally melted to a semiliquid state is known as lava. The speed of its flow depends on temperature, and the minerals it contains. One of the fastest lava flows ever measured was from the Nyiragongo volcano in the Democratic Republic of the Congo. It poured out at over 35 mph (60 km/h).

◀ Burning lava flows like a river, and boils the water as it enters the ocean.

Ash

Vast plumes of ash often erupt from a volcano, and can remain airborne for days—and travel great distances—before settling. When Mount Vesuvius erupted in AD 79, a huge column of pumice ash was ejected from the crater at a rate of 1.7 million tons per second. The column reached a height of 2 mi (3.3 km) before collapsing and covering the ground with a suffocating layer of ash.

Eruption

Volcanoes erupt when heat and pressure become too great for the crust to bear, and the huge amounts of energy below the surface are released. In the last of many eruptions in AD 186, a New Zealand volcano ejected an incredible 25 cubic mi (110 cubic km) of rock in one of the most violent eruptions ever recorded. Its crater is now Lake Taupo.

◀ Clouds of ash are carried upward by the force of exploding gas.

BENEATH THE SURFACE

Molten rock inside the Earth (magma) collects in chambers just below the surface. Heat and pressure force the magma upward, through weak areas in the crust, sometimes until it reaches the surface.

Vent

Conduit (main vent to the magma chamber)

Side vent

Upper magma chamber

Deep magma chamber

Mantle

Crater

A crater marks the opening of the vent. Lava builds up around it, creating the familiar cone shape. If the cone walls collapse, the crater will get bigger. The volcanoes of Hawaii are among the most active on Earth. Steam and volcanic gases pour out of their craters.

HOT Spots

I n some places, evidence of Earth's extraordinary inner heat comes to the surface. Soaring temperatures bake the rock underfoot, and boil water that lurks within it, causing jets of superheated steam to spurt into the air. Even mud can start to bubble!

Yellowstone

One third of the world's hydrothermal features are in Yellowstone Park in the U.S., which also has more geysers than anywhere else on Earth— 150 of them in just one square mile (2.6 sq km). The whole area sits astride a supervolcano, and while normal volcanoes make mountains, supervolcanoes explode them to smithereens. The most recent eruption was 640,000 years ago, and 1,000 times more powerful than the eruption of Mount St. Helens in 1980. The land continues to reach temperatures of 400°F (around 200°C), and new geysers, mud pools, and fumaroles are constantly created.

Old Faithful

The world's most famous geyser, Old Faithful of Yellowstone Park, U.S., shoots hot water and steam up to 180 ft (about 55 m) into the air. It erupts, on average, every 85–95 minutes because it takes this long for the chamber beneath to refill with water.

The greatest geyser

The tallest geyser ever witnessed existed for only four years, after a volcanic eruption in New Zealand in 1900. Waimangu's jets of black water, rocks, and steam were 1,500 ft (460 m) high—taller than the Empire State Building. Four tourists died in 1903 after being swept away by a sudden, and violent, eruption.

▶ Old Faithful is probably the world's most studied, and best-known, geyser.

▶ Macaques enjoy a hot soak so much they sometimes doze off in the pool.

Monkey baths

Warm water pools created by hot springs in Nagano, Japan, have been adopted by macaque monkeys. They bathe in these natural hot tubs during the freezing winter months.

Cotton Castle

At Pamukkale in Turkey, cascading pools create one of the world's most breathtaking natural wonders. The hot springs, which are rich in minerals, pour down the hillside, filling the pools with warm, blue water. The name Pamukkale means "Cotton Castle."

▶ Pamukkale's hot water pools are created by minerals in the hot water, which turn to stone.

THE GROUND IN SOME VOLCANIC REGIONS IS SO HOT IT CAN TURN MUD INTO BOILING POOLS, AS GASES RISE TO THE SURFACE AND BREAK THROUGH.

CRUNCH Time

Rock is tough but brittle, so it's no wonder that the active Earth, with all of its subterranean stirrings, puts the rocky landscape under more pressure than it can bear. When crunch time comes, giant sections of rock buckle and slip, creating monumental movements that cause Earth's surface to quake and shatter.

WHAT'S AT FAULT?

A fault is an enormous crack in Earth's crust, either side of which giant slabs of rock, called tectonic plates, move in different directions. As the slabs slide slowly past each other they may get stuck, causing a buildup of pressure that, when released, results in sudden jolts.

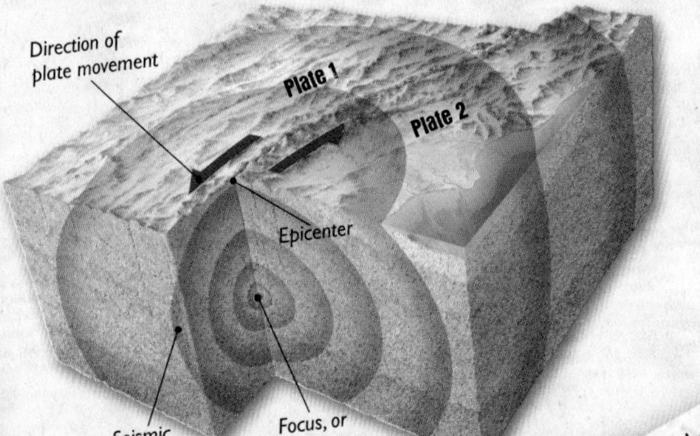

Direction of plate movement

Plate 1

Plate 2

Epicenter

Seismic waves

Focus, or hypocenter

▲ Massive movements along faults release energy around the focus. Seismic waves radiate outward, wreaking destruction in built-up areas.

IN 2010 A QUAKE IN CHILE WAS SO POWERFUL THAT IT LITERALLY MOVED THE ENTIRE CITY OF CONCEPCION 10 FT (3 M) TO THE WEST.

Locals walk along damaged roads as they are evacuated from the earthquake-hit Beichuan County, southwest China, in 2008.

Extreme damage

Major disaster

The 1906 San Francisco earthquake was caused by movement along the San Andreas fault.

Safety measures

A controlled explosion collapses a disused building, simulating an earthquake, and allowing scientists to test a "cage" (red) that would protect people inside.

Predicting quakes

Earthquakes are one of the most catastrophic of all extreme events, yet predicting them remains virtually impossible. Earthquake-proof construction, however, can save lives. Buildings in Japan and California, U.S., are constructed with elastic building materials and shock-absorbing foundations to withstand tremors.

Mega-tsunami

Seafloor shake-up

Tsunamis are caused by sudden, massive movements along fault lines on the seafloor. When faults are close to land, the chance of a mega-tsunami—a high wave of devastating proportions—is greatly increased.

The Indian Ocean mega-tsunami of 2004 devastated the Phi Phi Islands.

GREATEST River

Water from the glaciers and mountains of the Andes pours into the Amazon River at its source.

This waterfall on the Jari River brings water from Guyana's Highlands to the Amazon.

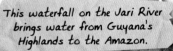

The Urubamba River is an Amazon headwater—a tributary forming part of the Amazon's source.

Rivers have the power to demolish walls of rock and grind them to dust. They have the strength to carry millions of tons of soil and sand, and enough energy to provide electricity for entire cities. There are long rivers, wide rivers, and deep rivers, but by almost any measure the Amazon is the greatest of them all.

A tributary is a river or stream that flows into a larger river. About 200 tributaries flow into the Amazon—more than any other river in the world.

TOP 5 RIVERS

The Nile is generally agreed to be slightly longer than the Amazon, but in terms of volume it's just a trickle by comparison. Every second, the Nile empties 6,600 yd³ (about 5,100 m³) of water into the sea, but the Amazon empties 290,000 yd³ (about 220,000 m³)—43 times as much. That is enough, in one day, to supply a city with fresh water for ten years!

PARANA
23,000 yd³ (about 17,700 m³) of water into the sea per second

YENISEI
25,000 yd³ (about 19,000 m³) of water into the sea per second

YANGTZE
42,000 yd³ (about 32,000 m³) of water into the sea per second

CONGO
55,000 yd³ (about 42,000 m³) of water into the sea per second

AMAZON
290,000 yd³ (about 220,000 m³) of water into the sea per second

During the wet season, the Amazon basin covers 135,000 sq mi (around 350,000 sq km)—an area similar to that of Germany. In the dry season it shrinks by two thirds.

WATER FROM THE AMAZON SUPPORTS THE AMAZON RAIN FOREST, WHICH COVERS 2 MILLION SQ MI (5 MILLION SQ KM). THAT'S TWO THIRDS OF THE AREA OF AUSTRALIA.

River dolphins live in the Amazon's slow-moving, muddy water. They feed on fish and crabs, but little is known about their behavior.

The area of land that is regularly covered by water following seasonal rains is called a floodplain.

THE AMAZON DELIVERS 106 MILLION CU FT (3 MILLION CU M) OF SEDIMENT INTO THE OCEAN EVERY DAY.

As it meets the ocean, extreme surfers take advantage of the unusually long waves (tidal bores) that occur here. It's possible to ride a single wave for 6 mi (10 km)!

The Amazon becomes the widest river on Earth near its mouth—up to 25 mi (40 km) wide in the wet season.

THE AMAZON HOLDS ABOUT 20 PERCENT OF THE WORLD'S TOTAL FRESH WATER.

Extreme EROSION

On our dynamic planet, nothing remains the same for long. The landscape is continually being molded, eroded, and changed by forces we are scarcely aware of. Human lives are too short for individuals to bear witness to these extraordinary processes, but the remarkable results are all around us.

▲ Hoodoos are tall columns of rock. The rock on the top of a column is harder than the rock beneath it.

A slot canyon is formed by rushing water passing through rock, and eroding a tall, narrow channel.

Sandblasting

In dry places, wind picks up grains of sand and whips them through the air like a sandblaster. The effects can be spectacular. In the Arches National Park of Utah, lofty monoliths, huge arches of rock, balancing rocks, and tablelike mesas stand as monuments in the desert.

▶ The Devil's Marbles, or balancing rocks, of Australia have been shaped by sandblasting.

WATER EROSION

The eroding power of the Colorado River is responsible for the Grand Canyon, one of the world's greatest natural wonders.

The Colorado River in the U.S. has proved itself the ultimate abrader of rock. Its erosive course began 17 million years ago—the blink of an eye in geological time. Since then it has created a canyon 277 mi (446 km) long, up to 18 mi (29 km) wide, and, in some places, more than one mile (1.6 km) deep, reaching rocks that are 2.5 billion years old.

The Colorado's enormous power of erosion is due to the river's great speed and volume, and the large amount of mud, sand, and gravel it carries. Also, the rocks through which it passes are relatively soft.

The Painted Cliffs in Tasmania are carved by wave erosion, and stained with orange-red minerals.

Breaking waves

In coastal areas, big waves crash against rocks and gradually wear them away in a process known as erosion. The ocean water not only has power and energy to do its work, it also carries grains of sand and mud, which rub away at the rock surfaces. Over time, cliffs are undercut, eventually collapsing into the ocean.

FREEZING Flow

In the world's coldest places snow falls but rarely melts. Layer upon layer of it collects, and the fluffy stuff is eventually compressed into dense packs of ice. Huge rivers of ice—glaciers—creep slowly downhill under the force of gravity. As they move, these heavyweight scourers carve a spectacular path through the landscape.

Ice cycles

Glacial ice is constantly melting and freezing, depending on the time of day, the season, and changing temperatures. When more ice freezes than melts, a glacier grows bigger and is said to be advancing. When ice is melting, a glacier shrinks and is described as retreating.

▲ Giant chunks of ice fall from the Perito Moreno glacier into Argentina's largest lake—Lago Argentino.

AGES OF ICE

The global climate is continually changing, and extreme climate changes that lead to ice ages are not unusual. In fact, we are probably experiencing a warm spell during a big ice age even now. During the last ice age so much water was trapped as ice that the world's sea levels fell by 300 ft (about 100 m).

MOST GLACIERS MOVE SLOWLY, BUT THE JAKOBSHAVN GLACIER IN GREENLAND IS REPUTED TO BE ONE OF THE FASTEST FLOWING, MOVING AT A RATE OF AROUND 65 FT (20 M) PER DAY.

▲ An artist's impression of the landscape and animals of the last Ice Age, about 10,000 years ago. Animals grew thick fur coats as protection against the cold. Many creatures, such as woolly mammoths, survived on plants such as mosses. Others, such as cave lions, were fierce hunters.

◄ The enormous Hubbard glacier reaches into the Gulf of Alaska. It has been slowly advancing for more than 100 years.

Icebergs

When ice sheets and glaciers meet the sea large sections may break off. These enormous frozen chunks float with ten percent of their mass above water because solid water is less dense than liquid water. Drifting icebergs are a hazard to shipping—it was an enormous iceberg that sank the liner *Titanic* in 1912, in which 1,517 people lost their lives.

THE ICECAP ON THE TOP OF MOUNT KILIMANJARO IN AFRICA IS MELTING SO FAST THAT IT MAY DISAPPEAR WITHIN THE NEXT 25 YEARS.

▼ A colony of penguins hitches a ride onboard an iceberg. They will dive back into the water and hunt for fish when they want to eat again.

A cruise ship is dwarfed by the massive Hubbard glacier

Enter the
ABYSS

A long-term drip of dissolved limestone can build up to create icicle-shaped stalactites

Deep underground, caverns and caves create dark and eerie natural theaters. Dramatic features adorn their walls, and tunnels extend far into Earth's hidden depths. Brave explorers who make the journey underground are often rewarded with awesome sights.

A sinking feeling

Acidic water can create a hole that descends vertically and creates an underwater waterfall. These sinkholes, as they are known, can form suddenly when large areas of weakened rock fall into caverns below. The result can be catastrophic when houses or roads collapse with them.

▼ This 30-story-deep sinkhole was caused by heavy rain during a hurricane in Guatemala.

▲ Drips of water fall to the cave floor and evaporate, and the solid minerals that are left behind build up over thousands of years, creating stalagmites.

Leaky limestone

Most underground caves form in karst landscapes—places where limestone is the dominant rock. As rain and river water seep through limestone it becomes acidic, and dissolves solid rock. The liquid it creates can turn back into limestone, creating stalactites, stalagmites, and other strange features.

Spelunkers

Caves are some of the least explored places on Earth, so there is a special thrill to be had from finding new caves and tunnels to navigate. People who undertake these often dangerous treks are known as spelunkers and pot-holers. The risks they have to be prepared for include cave collapse, hypothermia, falling, flooding, and getting lost.

AT OVER 390 MI (630 KM), MAMMOTH CAVE IN KENTUCKY, U.S., IS THE LONGEST CAVE SYSTEM IN THE WORLD.

▼ Giant crystals of aragonite, a form of calcium carbonate, may develop in some limestone cave systems.

▲ When exploring a cave system, spelunkers may be faced with long stretches of tiny tunnels as well as vast, impressive caverns.

Sizing it up

Cave experts have been mapping a cave network in Sarawak, Borneo, for more than 30 years. By taking measurements using lasers, they have gathered data on over 200 mi (320 km) of the Gunung Mulu network. It contains the world's largest cave—Sarawak Chamber is 2,300 ft (700 m) long and 330 ft (100 m) high.

▼ The gigantic Gunung Mulu caves were only discovered in 1976, beneath a rain forest.

Ancient history

The major mineral in limestone is calcium carbonate, which comes from the shells and skeletons of sea creatures. Over millions of years, the shells and skeletons collected on the seafloor and were, under great pressure, eventually turned into rock.

BURIED Treasure

E arth's crust contains a treasure trove of minerals that civilization depends upon. Many substances that we take for granted—iron, oil, gold, even talcum powder and the "lead" (graphite) in pencils—are formed in Earth's crust. Extracting them can demand feats of human endurance and technological wizardry.

MARBLE This smooth, strong stor is used in sculptur and buildings.

STEEL A tough metal made by mixing iron with other minerals.

ALUMINUM Strong but lightweight, this metal has many uses.

FLUORITE This pretty mineral is fluorescent (emits light) under ultraviolet light.

DEADLY COLTAN Coltan is a mineral used in the manufacture of cell phones, but extracting it is a life-threatening activity for people in the Democratic Republic of the Congo. Miners use their bare hands to dig, and risk facing collapsing mine shafts, radioactive minerals, and other deadly toxins.

HEMATITE Ground up, this mineral makes a red paint used since prehistory.

MERCURY This liquid metal is used in thermometers to measure temperature.

GRAPHITE Its flexible network of carbon atoms makes graphite very soft.

COAL Burning this fossil fuel releases heat and light energy.

IN DEEP WATER

When the *Deepwater Horizon* rig exploded in 2010 it killed ten men, sparked the world's largest accidental oil spill, and caused environmental catastrophes. The rig was built to research a reservoir of oil on an area of the seafloor beneath 5,000 ft (about 1,520 m) of water, a challenge that has been described as being more technically difficult than exploring the Moon.

▲ The explosion of the oil rig *Deepwater Horizon* on April 20, 2010 caused an estimated 5 million barrels—210 million gal (800 million l)—of oil to spill into the Gulf of Mexico.

GOLD LEAF Gold is an amazing metal that can be worked more readily than any other. Just 0.03 oz (1 g) can be beaten into 10 sq ft (1 sq m).

NICKEL This silvery metal is used in coins and batteries.

CROWN JEWELS The greatest working collection of jewels includes the Imperial Crown of India, which contains over 6,000 diamonds.

COPPER Can be beaten or rolled into shape, and conducts electricity very well.

DIAMOND Diamonds are made of carbon, which in another form becomes the soft graphite in a pencil lead. It is the hardest known natural mineral, and the most brilliant when cut.

GYPSUM Can be heated to make plaster, used in building, or made into blackboard chalk.

Deep-sea DIVE

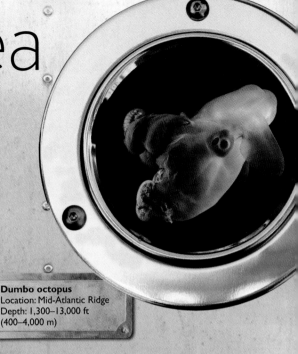

The deep ocean is the world's least explored and most mysterious environment. It is a high-pressure, dark wilderness, so hostile to life that few creatures can survive there. Those that can are bizarre, ranging from colossal squid with eyes bigger than a human head, to glow-in-the-dark fish, and giant worms.

Dumbo octopus
Location: Mid-Atlantic Ridge
Depth: 1,300–13,000 ft
(400–4,000 m)

Journey to the bottom of the sea

In 1960 two explorers, Jacques Piccard and Don Walsh, embarked on one of the most treacherous journeys ever undertaken. Their submersible, the *Trieste*, took them 35,800 ft (10,900 m) into the Mariana Trench, the deepest point of any ocean. To this day they remain the only two people to have made the journey. By contrast, 12 people have traveled to the Moon, which is 238,600 mi (384,000 km) away.

Snow and ooze

Bits of detritus from dead animals and plants are known as marine snow. They drift down to the deep seabed and, over time, build up to create enormous sediments of fine mud and ooze. Some of them are 1,480 ft (450 m) thick.

DeepSee submersible
Carries up to three people to depths of 1,500 ft (about 460 m).

▶ The mineral-rich geysers of water that come from the seabed are called black smokers, and can reach temperatures of 750°F (400°C).

Oasis undersea

The deep sea is a poor habitat for most wildlife, but some places are able to support some of the world's strangest fauna. Fueled by volcanic heat that escapes from cracks in Earth's crust, hydrothermal vents can sustain colonies of limpets, shrimps, starfish, tube worms, and fish.

Giant ostracod
Location: Mid-Atlantic Ridge
Depth: 2,356–6,115 ft
(718–1,864 m)

The future

Researching the deep ocean remains one of the great challenges facing science. It is such a perilous environment that humans rarely venture there. ROVs (remotely operated vehicles), such as *Jason*, and AUVs (autonomous underwater vehicles), such as *Sentry*, are now used to enable scientists to explore the seabed from the safety of a ship's deck above.

◀ This image uses colors to show the uneven nature of the Pacific Ocean seabed. The deepest areas appear blue and green. Underwater peaks appear as red and yellow, and mark the East Pacific Rise.

ZONES OF THE DEEP

0 ft

Light Zone Sunlight travels through the water at this level, so plants can photosynthesize (make food), supporting a large range of life-forms.

650 ft

Twilight Zone Dim levels of light can pass through the water, but there is not enough light to support photosynthesis.

3,300 ft

Dark Zone Many animals survive in the inky depths. The seabed is home to sponges, shelled animals, sea cucumbers, and worms.

13,000 ft

Abyssal Zone Fewer animals can survive as the water gets deeper. A great pressure of water bears down on those that do.

20,000 ft

Hadal Zone This is the most mysterious place on Earth, and some strange creatures manage to survive here. Little is known about them.

WILD
Winds

Wind is little more than moving air. It is invisible and almost weightless—yet it is impossible to control and is one of the planet's most destructive forces. When winds become high-energy storms, they can develop into hurricanes more than 500 mi (800 km) across—and wreak total havoc.

◀ A spinning tornado collects dirt and grit from the land, turning it into a brown funnel of air.

ON APRIL 3, 1974, THE U.S. ENDURED WHAT IS THOUGHT TO HAVE BEEN ITS WORST EVER TORNADO OUTBREAK, DURING WHICH 150 TORNADOES CAUSED MORE THAN 300 DEATHS AND 6,000 STORM-RELATED INJURIES.

A supercell storm, such as this one in Nebraska, U.S., can produce several tornadoes during a few hours of activity.

Twisting tornadoes

Tornadoes can be deadly, but short-lived. They begin when warm, wet air encounters cool, dry air. In the right circumstances, a vertical column of rotating air forms, which causes a "supercell" that can transform into vortex of violently rotating wind.

On the move

Air moves because it becomes warm in some places, and cool in others. Warm air molecules have more energy, and move faster, than cold ones. When air moves faster, it expands and rises above cold air, setting up weather systems that sometimes have extreme outcomes.

Storm chasers

Tornado Alley in the Great Plains region of the U.S. is famous for its wild winds, and the storm chasers that pursue them for the thrill, or to gather scientific data. Storm chasers don't just watch the twisters—their goal is to actually go inside them. They follow computer weather models and search for brewing storms. Once in the middle of a tornado, storm chasers rely on their vehicles for protection against high-speed winds, torrential rain, lightning, and giant hailstones.

Hurricanes

The world's greatest storms are called hurricanes, typhoons, or tropical cyclones. They begin at sea and can inflict terrible damage if they move onto land. The worst hurricanes have winds that swirl at more than 155 mph (250 km/h). At this velocity, winds have the strength to rip the roofs off buildings and cause storm surges, when seawater is picked up and hurled inland.

On August 29, 2005, Hurricane Katrina hit land, causing devastating damage in areas such as Kenner, Louisiana, U.S.

IN 1900, A HURRICANE BARRELED THE TEXAN CITY OF GALVESTON, FLATTENING IT AND CAUSING A STORM SURGE AND ONE OF THE U.S.'S WORST NATURAL DISASTERS. AS MANY AS 10,000 PEOPLE DIED IN ONE NIGHT.

Freaky
WEATHER

Weird weather events have long been features of biblical tales and folklore, and have often been attributed to a divine intervention in earthly matters. Scientists have sought to uncover the genuine causes of these oddities, and today they are more likely to be explained by rare, but entirely natural, weather systems.

Cloud art

The study of clouds is called nephology, and for many people it is more of an art than a science. These airborne masses hold water droplets or ice crystals and, owing to climatic conditions, can form some strange shapes. Freaky cloud formations include mushrooms, jellyfish, and donuts!

◀ These puffy clouds, known as mammatus, hang beneath the main body of other clouds and often precede violent storms.

Sun halo

Also called a sundog, this strange atmospheric phenomenon is caused by ice crystals inside high, thin clouds. The crystals reflect light, causing it to shine in a ring, and creating a rainbow that looks as if it is wrapped around the Sun.

Raining fish and frogs

For centuries there have been reports of strange things falling from the sky during storms. These bizarre events are caused by tornadoes, or their watery equivalents—waterspouts. Animals, especially fish or frogs, are swept up into the air, carried some distance, and then dropped during a rainstorm.

▶ A waterspout forms and touches down alongside the Mekong River in Cambodia.

A CHUNK OF ICE MEASURING 7 IN (NEARLY 18 CM) ACROSS FELL FROM THE SKY DURING A STORM IN AURORA, NEBRASKA, U.S., IN 2003.

◀ Lightning striking through a column of volcanic ash produces a dazzling display.

Blue Moon

The Moon may appear blue when forest fires or volcanic ash send tiny particles into the atmosphere where they mix with droplets of water. The mixture is carried by winds and refracts moonlight, causing a blue haze to form.

Fiendish fireballs

About 100 lightning strikes occur around the world every second, slashing through the sky with awesome electrical energy. Balls of lightning, however, are rare events. Fireballs can be the size of a beach ball and they have been seen to pass through windows and walls, hiss, and even explode.

BLUE AND RED FLASHES OF LIGHT ARE KNOWN AS BLUE JETS AND RED SPRITES AND ARE SOMETIMES SEEN ABOVE STORMS. THEY ARE PROBABLY CAUSED BY LIGHTNING IN THE UPPER REGIONS OF THE EARTH'S ATMOSPHERE.

▼ In 2010 parts of Queensland, Australia, were hit by flood waters that covered an area larger than France and Germany put together.

Freak floods

Flooding is one of the most common natural disasters on Earth, but flash floods take everyone by surprise. Often caused by a break in flood defenses or riverbanks, following unusually heavy rains or ice-melts, flash floods swamp large areas. In low-lying areas, the effects can be particularly catastrophic.

Ultra FREEZE

Soft, fluffy snow can transform a landscape into a stunning, white wilderness. Yet in its most extreme forms, snow can also bring disaster and destruction. From raging blizzards to colossal avalanches that crash to the ground with the impact of solid rock, the power of snow should never be underestimated.

MOUNT BAKER IN WASHINGTON STATE IN THE U.S. HAD A TOTAL SNOWFALL OF 95 FT (29 M) IN THE WINTER OF 1998–1999.

What is snow?

In cold places—mostly near Earth's poles or at high altitude—rising water vapor can freeze as tiny ice particles in the air. Ice crystals stick together to form snowflakes. The simplest snowflakes are six-sided prisms, but these can branch to create more complex structures. The shape and size of a snowflake depends on the temperature, pressure, and amount of water that is held in the air.

Is every snowflake unique?

Probably yes, although how would anyone ever know? If several trillion ice crystals fell every year, the chance of two identical crystals forming in the lifetime of the Universe is virtually zero.

AVALANCHE SURVIVAL

Mountain rescuers recommend some simple steps to increase the likelihood of survival when out in avalanche-prone areas.

* Check avalanche hotlines and assess the avalanche risk before going into an area.
* If you are skiing or snowboarding, carry an avalanche rescue beacon, which transmits a message to rescue teams.
* You can't outrun an avalanche, but you may be able to run to the side of one.

* If you are knocked off your feet, grab hold of a tree or a rock, or stick your ski pole into the snow.
* Being caught by an avalanche is like being caught in river rapids—the snow will start to pull you under. Try to "swim" through it, and keep trying to make your way to the top of the snow pile.

* When you stop tumbling, clear an area in front of your face so you can breathe.
* Push your arm upward for the best chance of being spotted by someone.
* If you see someone being caught by an avalanche, mark the last point you saw them, so that you—or a rescue team—have a better chance of finding them.

Whiteout

A blizzard is a snowstorm driven by winds of 30 mph (48 km/h) or more, where visibility is reduced to 650 ft (200 m) or less. In a severe blizzard or "whiteout," visibility is near to zero.

A SEASON OF BLIZZARDS IN WESTERN U.S. IN 1949 LASTED FOR SEVEN WEEKS. DURING THAT TIME MORE THAN 100 PEOPLE, AND ONE MILLION CATTLE, DIED.

Hundreds of tons of snow coursing down a hillside can fell trees, crush cars, and demolish houses.

DANGER AVALANCHE

Alpine avalanche

Heavy snow in Chamonix, France, in 1999 caused an avalanche of more than 10.6 million cubic ft (300,000 cubic m) of snow. The flow traveled at 60 mph (97 km/h) until it hit a small hamlet below, destroying buildings and burying people under 100,000 tons of snow. Twelve people died.

The Arctic is a frozen ocean surrounded by continents. During the height of summer in the Arctic Circle, daylight continues for 24 hours. In winter, there is at least one day when the Sun does not rise.

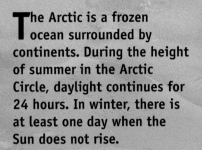

◀▲ Animals that can survive within the Arctic Circle include Arctic foxes and polar bears. The foxes often follow the bears, to feed on the leftover bits of their kills.

▲ Divers explore under Arctic ice, discovering wildlife that survives at the Earth's extreme ends.

The Ends of
THE EARTH

▶ Animals that can survive in the Antarctic include penguins, seals, whales, and albatross. Shrimplike krill live in the Southern Ocean and are among the most numerous animals on the planet.

The South Pole is on a massive continent—Antarctica—which is covered by the world's largest icecap. With an average area of 5.3 million sq mi (13.7 million sq km), the icecap is one-and-a-half times bigger than the U.S., and holds about 70 percent of the world's fresh water.

▼ Scientists explore ice caves in Antarctica to uncover the region's mysterious past.

A time-delay photograph captures the midnight sun and its reflection in the Arctic Ocean, as it appears to move across the sky.

IN 1958, A SUBMARINE SAILED BENEATH THE FROZEN ARCTIC OCEAN, PROVING THE ICE SHEET RESTS ON WATER, NOT ON LAND.

Temperatures in northern Greenland can fall to −94°F (−70°C).

NORTH POLE

SOUTH POLE

IN PARTS OF THE ANTARCTIC THE SUN REMAINS BELOW THE HORIZON FOR 105 DAYS DURING THE WINTER, LEAVING THE LAND IN NEAR-TOTAL DARKNESS.

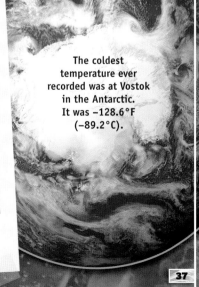

The coldest temperature ever recorded was at Vostok in the Antarctic. It was −128.6°F (−89.2°C).

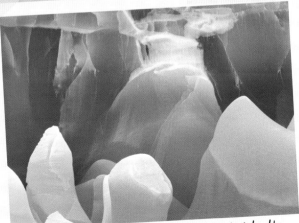

In winter, the Antarctic ice sheet spreads into the ocean, forming layers called ice shelves. Huge ice blocks break off the shelves to form massive icebergs.

Super DRY

Deserts are the world's driest places, where years may pass with no rain at all. They can also suffer extremes of temperature, with hot days and freezing nights. Even the icy Antarctic is classed as a desert. These super-dry places are desolate and often barren—without access to water, few living things can survive.

EARTH'S HOTTEST PLACES

1 Al'Azizíya, Libya
135.9°F (57.7°C)

2 Greenland Ranch, Death Valley, U.S.
134°F (56.7°C)

3 Ghudamis, Libya and Kebili, Tunisia
131°F (55°C)

Las Vegas is a city of excess, but scientists warn it could run dry in the next 50 years.

The desert city

Despite the harsh and inhospitable environment of deserts, one of the world's most successful cities was built in one. Las Vegas, in the American Mohave Desert, is home to 1.8 million people and accommodates 30 million tourists a year. Water is supplied by nearby Lake Mead, but the city is growing too fast for the supply.

In Los Angeles, 140 gal (530 l) a day is required per person—in Las Vegas that figure swells to an unsustainable 307 gal (1,165 l).

A fast-moving wall of Saharan sand and dust, called a haboob, advances on a market in Sudan.

Scorched Sahara

The giant Sahara Desert covers an area equivalent to the U.S., and it is growing all the time. Huge dunes form, reaching heights of 970 ft (300 m), and winds can whip up sandstorms and dust devils. Dust is lighter than sand, and can travel enormous distances.

ARICA IN THE CHILEAN ATACAMA DESERT EXPERIENCED LESS THAN 0.03 IN (0.75 MM) OF RAIN DURING ONE 59-YEAR PERIOD.

Burning up

Wildfires are often started by human activity or lightning strikes, and when they take hold in areas that have endured long, dry periods they can spread by leaps and bounds. Australia has about 15,000 wildfires a year. In 1997, strong winds followed a severe drought in Indonesia, and the result was a massive inferno that raged across 2,900 sq mi (7,500 sq km).

◀ Known as bushfires in Australia, these infernos can rampage through 12 mi (20 km) of vegetation in just one hour.

EARTH'S DRIEST PLACES

RAINFALLS, ON AVERAGE

1. ARICA, CHILE
   ONE DAY EVERY SIX YEARS

2. ASYÛT, EGYPT
   ONE DAY EVERY FIVE YEARS

3. DAKHLA OASIS, EGYPT
   ONE DAY EVERY FOUR YEARS

INDEX